EAST LAKE ELEMENTARY SCHOOL
4715 162ND ST W
LAKEVILLE, MINNESOTA 55044

D0938605

SAN DIEGO
PADRES

by Bernie Wilson

SportsZone

An Imprint of Abdo Publishing
www.abdopublishing.com

www.abdopublishing.com

Published by Abdo Publishing, a division of ABDO, PO Box 398166, Minneapolis, Minnesota 55439. Copyright © 2015 by Abdo Consulting Group, Inc. International copyrights reserved in all countries. No part of this book may be reproduced in any form without written permission from the publisher. SportsZone™ is a trademark and logo of Abdo Publishing.

Printed in the United States of America, North Mankato, Minnesota
052014
092014

THIS BOOK CONTAINS
RECYCLED MATERIALS

Editor: Melissa York
Copy Editor: Nicholas Cafarelli
Interior Design and Production: Carol Castro
Cover Design: Kazuko Collins

Photo Credits: Darron Cummings/AP Images, cover; Al Behrman/AP Images, 40, 43 (bottom); Lenny Ignelzi/AP Images, title, 29, 34, 36, 43 (middle); Thane McIntosh/The San Diego Union Tribune/Getty Images, 4, 42 (bottom); Ronald C. Modra/Sports Imagery/Getty Images, 7, 9; George Gojkovich/Getty Images, 10; AP Images, 13, 42 (top); G. Paul Burnett/AP Images, 14; Fred Jewell/AP Images, 16, 42 (middle); Jack Smith/AP Images, 19; Bernstein Associates/Getty Images, 20; John Gastaldo/AP Images, 23; Mike Poche/AP Images, 25, 43 (top); David J. Phillip/AP Images, 26; Robert Sullivan/AFP/Getty Images, 30; Eric Draper/AP Images, 33; Kevork Djansezian/AP Images, 38; Charlie Riedel/AP Images, 44; Chris Park/AP Images, 47

Library of Congress Control Number: 2014933085
Cataloging-in-Publication Data
Wilson, Bernie.
  San Diego Padres / by Bernie Wilson.
      p. cm. -- (Inside MLB)
  Includes bibliographical references and index.
  ISBN 978-1-62403-483-1
  1. San Diego Padres (Baseball team : National League of Professional Baseball Clubs)--History--Juvenile literature. I. Title.
  GV875.S33W55 2015
  796.357'6409794985--dc23
                                        2014933085

TABLE OF CONTENTS

CHAPTER 1

A WORLD SERIES AT LAST

Steve Garvey took a mighty swing and drove the ball through the San Diego night. It landed beyond the fence in right field, setting off a huge celebration. Garvey had hit a two-run home run in the ninth inning off star relief pitcher Lee Smith. The hit gave the Padres a 7–5 win over the Chicago Cubs.

The victory evened the 1984 National League Championship Series (NLCS) at two games apiece, but the home run was not quite enough to get the Padres to the World Series. They would clinch their first National League (NL) pennant the next afternoon after a Cubs error. But Garvey's shot had finally given the Padres a defining moment after years buried in last place. It remains perhaps the biggest moment in franchise history. After all, 1984 was only the second time in its history that the team had a winning record. And it was hard for some people to take the team seriously. Its team

Steve Garvey celebrates with his teammates after hitting the game-winning home run in Game 4 of the 1984 NLCS.

colors of brown and yellow were even a joke, often referred to as "mustard and mud."

Garvey had been a star with the rival Los Angeles Dodgers. He joined the Padres as a free agent at the start of the 1983 season. That it was a former Dodger who saved the Padres' season made the home run even more remarkable.

The Padres were led by hard-nosed manager Dick Williams. They won their first NL West title in 1984. Their record of 92–70 earned them a berth against the Cubs in the NLCS. There were only two divisions at that time, so the two division winners played for the pennant. It looked as though the Cubs were going to embarrass the Padres. Chicago won the opener 13–0 in the friendly confines of Wrigley Field. They hit five home runs while keeping the Padres scoreless. The next afternoon, the Cubs won 4–2. It seemed as though it would be a quick series.

The Padres flew home to San Diego. They could hardly believe their eyes when their buses pulled into the parking lot at Jack Murphy Stadium. They were greeted by thousands of cheering, hopeful fans. Two nights later, the Padres played the first home playoff game in team history. It was

The Garv

Steve Garvey was known for two things—his muscular forearms and his position as the star first baseman with the Los Angeles Dodgers. He had been a fixture with the Dodgers since the early 1970s, helping them reach four World Series. When his contract expired after the 1982 season, he became one of the top free agents on the market. The Padres made the strongest push for him. For some fans, it was odd seeing a former rival wearing a Padres uniform. After his landmark home run in the NLCS, however, he cemented his place in Padres history.

Padres pitcher Rich "Goose" Gossage pitches during Game 3 of the NLCS against the Chicago Cubs.

a beauty. Cheered by a sellout crowd, the Padres won 7–1. Ed Whitson's pitching and Kevin McReynolds's three-run home run led the team to victory. The momentum clearly had shifted.

The next night, it was Garvey's turn to shine. He finished 4-for-5 with five runs batted in (RBIs), including his famous home run. The series went to the deciding Game 5, and the Padres did not disappoint their loyal fans. The Cubs took a 3–0 lead, but the Padres came back. The game turned on a Tim Flannery grounder. The ball went through first

Boch and Flan

Two members of the 1984 Padres went on to long careers managing and coaching in the big leagues. Bruce Bochy was a backup catcher and Tim Flannery was an infielder. Flannery became a fan favorite with his scrappy play. Both went on to coach and manage in the minor league system before returning to San Diego as coaches. Bochy was the third-base coach until he was promoted to manager prior to the 1995 season. He led the Padres to four division titles and one World Series. He moved on to the San Francisco Giants after the 2006 season. Flannery was Bochy's third-base coach in San Diego for several seasons and followed him to the Giants. In 2010, Bochy led the Giants to a World Series win.

baseman Leon Durham's legs for an error, bringing in the tying run. Tony Gwynn then stepped to the plate and ripped a double past second baseman Ryne Sandberg. The hit gave the Padres a 5–3 lead. Garvey hit a single to drive in Gwynn and set the final score at 6–3.

The entire city went wild as fans celebrated the team's first trip to the World Series.

The red-hot Detroit Tigers were waiting for them in the World Series. The Tigers had finished the regular season with the best record in baseball, 104–58. They won three straight games against Kansas City in the American League (AL) Championship Series. They came to San Diego and quickly won the World Series opener 3–2. The Padres won the second game 5–3 with a three-run home run from Kurt Bevacqua. After that, the highlights dried up. The Tigers wrapped it up by winning the next three games back in Detroit. Detroit slugger Kirk Gibson and shortstop Alan Trammell led the way. Trammell, a San Diego native, was named World Series Most Valuable Player (MVP).

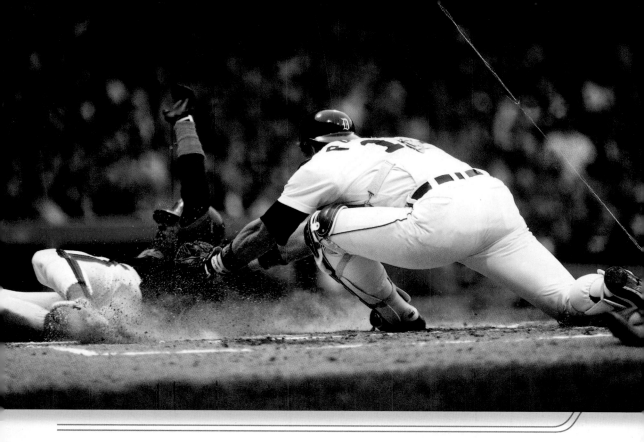

Padres second baseman Alan Wiggins is tagged out at home plate during Game 5 of the 1984 World Series.

The Padres returned home to San Diego and headed into the off-season. Gwynn and others thought there would be more World Series trips in the team's immediate future. Instead, it would be 14 long years before Padres made it back to the Fall Classic.

Tony's Sweet Spot

The Padres were loaded with stars in 1984, including right fielder Tony Gwynn. The left-hander had a sweet batting stroke. He loved hitting the ball to the opposite field. He was particularly adept at hitting the ball between third base and shortstop. Third base is denoted as position number five by scorekeepers and shortstop is position number six. Gwynn nicknamed his favorite spot the "5.5 hole."

CHAPTER 2

FROM THE MINORS TO THE MAJORS

The NL approved the addition of the expansion Padres and Montreal Expos for the 1969 season. However, there already had been a San Diego Padres team in existence since 1936.

Those Padres were part of the minor league Pacific Coast League (PCL). They played in a cozy little ballpark down by the harbor, Lane Field. One of the early stars of that team was San Diego native Ted Williams. He later starred with the Boston Red Sox.

The PCL Padres were popular. But San Diego civic and sports leaders were hungry to have a major league team. The city was already home to the National Football League's Chargers, who had been playing in San Diego since 1961. Their wish was finally granted. The new Padres began play at San Diego Stadium in 1969. They were named after the Franciscan friars who founded San

Hall of Famer Dave Winfield played for the Padres from 1973 to 1980. He retired in 1995 after 22 seasons in the major leagues.

Diego in 1769. The stadium, coincidentally, was located on Friars Road. They were owned by businessman C. Arnholt Smith, who had owned the PCL Padres.

Unfortunately, the early Padres were not very good. They had big-name players such as first baseman Nate Colbert, pitcher Randy Jones, and right fielder Dave Winfield. But, the Padres lost 100 or more games four times in their first six seasons. They posted a losing record in each of their first nine seasons. They failed to post a winning record until their tenth season, in 1978, when they finished 84–78. That was only good for fourth place in the NL West.

Still, the Padres had their share of big performances. Colbert was their first slugger. He hit 38 home runs in 1970 and again in 1972. He once clubbed five home runs and drove in 13 runs in a doubleheader at Atlanta.

New trouble began when they had existed for only five seasons. Smith wanted to sell the team to a grocery store owner named Joseph Danzansky. He planned to move the team to Washington DC. The deal seemed all but done when city officials said the Padres still had 15 seasons remaining

Padres owner Ray Kroc stands behind the center field fence at San Diego Stadium on April 12, 1979.

on their stadium lease. That caused the deal to fall through. It was at this moment that McDonald's restaurant cofounder Ray Kroc stepped up. Kroc bought the team to keep it in San Diego.

Kroc became enormously popular for saving the Padres. He also earned a spot in team lore for what he said on opening night, April 9, 1974. Over

No No-Hitters

Through the 2013 season, no Padres pitcher had ever thrown a no-hitter. Some people blame it on the curse of Clay Kirby. On July 21, 1970, Kirby held the New York Mets hitless through eight innings. Surprisingly, manager Preston Gomez had Cito Gaston pinch hit for Kirby. Reliever Jack Baldschun allowed a single to open the ninth and the Padres lost 3–0. Several Padres have come close to no-hitters, but none have succeeded.

The San Diego Chicken performed for fans at ballparks throughout the country. Padres owner and McDonald's cofounder Ray Kroc used the mascot in McDonald's television commercials.

The San Diego Chicken

One of the most famous mascots in the history of sports is the San Diego Chicken. Ted Giannoulas dressed in a red chicken suit and entertained fans on behalf of a local radio station, KGB-FM Radio, beginning in 1974. He soon began appearing at events across the country. His antics have amused fans and annoyed players and coaches for many years.

the stadium public address system, Kroc thanked the fans for their support. But he was frustrated by the way his Padres were playing against the Houston Astros. "Fans, I suffer with you," he said. "I've never seen such stupid ballplaying in my life." The fans roared their approval.

However, some players were not amused by Kroc's

speech. Astros player Doug Rader said, "He thinks he's in a sales convention dealing with a bunch of his short-order cooks." So, the next time the Astros came to town, Kroc held a short-order cook's night. Any fan wearing a short-order cook's hat got in free. Rader delivered the Astros' lineup card to home plate on a platter while wearing a short-order cook's hat.

The Padres still did not have many winning seasons in the mid- to late-1970s. But they began to produce star players. Jones became a workhorse. He won the NL Cy Young Award in 1976. He had a 22–14 record and 2.74 earned-run average (ERA). In 1978, Gaylord Perry won the Cy Young Award with a 21–6 record and 2.73 ERA.

Winfield was a slugging outfielder. He went straight from the University of Minnesota to the Padres in 1973. Very

Hall of Famers

Dave Winfield was the first player to go into the National Baseball Hall of Fame with a Padres cap on his plaque. He spent the first eight seasons of his career with San Diego. In a 22-year career with six teams, he had 3,110 hits and 465 home runs. He drove in the winning run in Game 6 of the 1992 World Series to lift the Toronto Blue Jays to their first championship. Other Hall of Famers who played for the Padres during their careers include Rollie Fingers, Gaylord Perry, Willie McCovey, Ozzie Smith, Rich "Goose" Gossage, Rickey Henderson, and Tony Gwynn. Former manager Dick Williams also was inducted into the Hall of Fame.

few players get to the majors without spending time in the minor leagues. Shortstop Ozzie Smith was with the Padres from 1978 to 1981. Although Winfield and Smith became stars for other teams, they honed their skills in San Diego. It would take the arrival of another baseball legend to finally bring the Padres into contention.

CHAPTER 3

MR. PADRE BOOSTS THE PADRES

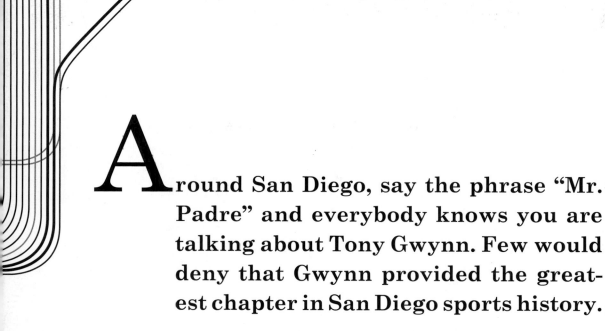

Around San Diego, say the phrase "Mr. Padre" and everybody knows you are talking about Tony Gwynn. Few would deny that Gwynn provided the greatest chapter in San Diego sports history.

Gwynn spent less than two seasons in the minor leagues. He would play for the Padres for 20 seasons. He made his big-league debut on July 19, 1982. His first hit was a double that night against the Philadelphia Phillies. Pete Rose, baseball's hit king, told Gwynn after the play, "Don't catch me all in one night, kid."

Gwynn became one of several stars on a team that was put together by general manager Jack McKeon. McKeon made so many trades that he was nicknamed "Trader Jack." McKeon signed closer Rich "Goose" Gossage as a free agent before the 1984 season. The lineup that season included Gwynn, Steve Garvey, second

Hall of Famer Tony Gwynn was one of the most accomplished hitters in the history of the game. He led the NL in batting average eight times.

baseman Alan Wiggins, third baseman Graig Nettles, shortstop Garry Templeton, and outfielders Kevin McReynolds and Carmelo Martinez. Playing for tough manager Dick Williams, the Padres finished with a 92–70 record.

The Padres endured a disappointing World Series loss in 1984 and stumbled badly during the next four seasons. They bounced back in 1989 before finishing three games out of first place. Closer Mark Davis became the third Padres pitcher to win the NL Cy Young Award. However, Davis left as a free agent in the off-season.

The Padres seemed poised for a comeback in the early 1990s. Joe McIlvaine was the general manager. In December 1990, he acquired shortstop Tony Fernandez and first baseman Fred McGriff from the Toronto Blue Jays. He traded away two popular players, outfielder Joe Carter and second baseman Roberto Alomar. However, San Diego responded by going 84–78 to finish third in the NL West.

Late in spring training of 1992, McIlvaine acquired third baseman Gary Sheffield from the Milwaukee Brewers. The Padres played well that season.

Padres slugger Tony Gwynn takes a swing during the 1992 All-Star Game.

When the Padres hosted the All-Star Game, they were represented by Gwynn, McGriff, Fernandez, Sheffield, and catcher Benito Santiago. Just as quickly, though, hope started fading. The ownership group wanted to cut salary. The first move was to trade pitcher Craig Lefferts. Another third-place finish gave the owners a reason to start making big changes.

RAK

The Padres played the 1984 season with the initials RAK on the left sleeve of the jerseys as a tribute to owner Ray Albert Kroc. Kroc had died of heart failure at age 81 on January 14, 1984, before the start of the season. Kroc did not live long enough to see his Padres reach their first World Series. Kroc's fun-loving personality made him stand out, even though his team did not always shine—at least until 1984, when it all came together.

CHAPTER 4

RISING FROM THE ASHES

The summer of 1993 was tough for Padres fans. It will forever be known as the Fire Sale. The Padres' ownership group traded several star players. They wanted to reduce the player payroll and save money.

The dealing actually began the summer before, when Craig Lefferts was sent to the Baltimore Orioles. It continued during the winter, when star shortstop Tony Fernandez was moved to the New York Mets. During the summer, a series of shocking trades saw sluggers Gary Sheffield and Fred McGriff and pitchers Bruce Hurst and Greg Harris leave town.

Sheffield had won the NL batting championship the previous season. McGriff had won the home-run title. It was only the third time in major league history that both a defending batting champion and home-run champion were traded the following season. The Padres ended up getting little value for McGriff. The trade for Sheffield was unpopular as well. General

Padres third baseman Gary Sheffield won the NL batting title in 1992 with a .330 average.

manager Randy Smith had been on the job for just a few weeks. He kept telling fans the Padres had received "value for value" in getting rookie reliever Trevor Hoffman from Florida. But few believed him at first.

It was a miserable summer. Tony Gwynn and pitcher Andy Benes were surrounded by a supporting cast of no-name players. The Padres lost 101 games, finishing 43 games behind the Atlanta Braves in the NL West. There was little hope for the next season too. The Padres were building for the mid-1990s.

It turns out that the Padres did receive value for value in the Hoffman trade. He eventually became baseball's all-time leader in saves. It just took a few seasons and a huge trade to turn the Padres back toward a winning record. When the players went on strike in August 1994, the Padres had the worst record in the major leagues, 47–70. Because of the strike, baseball commissioner Bud Selig called off the season and the World Series.

Two events helped turn the Padres back into winners. On December 21, 1994, computer software tycoon John Moores became majority owner. He bought the team from

Pitcher Andy Benes had one All-Star season (1993) during his tenure with the Padres from 1989 to 1995.

CAMMY

Ken Caminiti was known as Cammy to teammates and fans. He was one of the toughest players in Padres history. He had the body of a football linebacker and always played hard, even when he was hurt. He was capable of snapping a bat over his knee after striking out. He looked fierce with his bushy goatee, but he was actually quiet and kindhearted. Caminiti was the unanimous choice as NL MVP in 1996. He led the team with 40 home runs and set a team record by driving in 130 runs. A terrific third baseman, he was also a switch-hitter, meaning he could bat right-handed or left-handed. He won the NL Gold Glove Award every season from 1995 to 1997. His legacy was tarnished when he later admitted he took steroids during his MVP season to help him deal with a shoulder injury. He also battled alcohol and drug addictions. Caminiti died of an overdose on October 10, 2004, three years after his career ended.

Hollywood producer Tom Werner and his group of investors. Werner had bought the team from Ray Kroc's wife, Joan, in 1990. A week after Moores bought the team, Smith swung a 12-player trade with the Houston Astros. It was one of the biggest deals in major league history. The Padres obtained third baseman Ken Caminiti, center fielder Steve Finley, and four other players.

With a new core of stars surrounding Gwynn, the Padres finished an encouraging 70–74 in 1995. In 1996, the Padres signed Rickey Henderson to bat leadoff and steal bases. He immediately became a fan favorite. They also added slugger Greg Vaughn at the trading deadline. Those deals helped set up an exciting season. It culminated with their first NL West title since 1984. The division race came

Third baseman Ken Caminiti, shown making a diving catch, was the NL MVP in 1996 and won the Gold Glove from 1995 to 1997 for his defense.

down to a final three-game series against the Dodgers in Los Angeles, which the Padres swept. Gwynn's younger brother, Chris, doubled in the winning run in the final game. Hoffman earned a save in all three games.

Although they went on to lose three straight games to the St. Louis Cardinals in the playoffs, the foundation had been laid. Baseball was fun again in San Diego. Caminiti established himself as a superstar third baseman. He was the unanimous choice for the 1996 NL MVP Award.

San Diego struggled in 1997. The team became the first defending NL West champion to drop to last place. Fortunately, it turned out to be a temporary setback.

CHAPTER 5

ANOTHER
WORLD SERIES

Poor pitching cost the Padres in 1997. So, general manager Kevin Towers made some quick changes. He gave the fans an early holiday present when he obtained ace Kevin Brown in a deal with the defending World Series champion Florida Marlins in December 1997.

Brown was stunned that the Marlins were dismantling their championship team. However, he came to San Diego and pitched with his usual tenacity. The Padres proved to be contenders from the start and dominated the NL West. With Brown leading the way, the pitching staff also got big contributions from Andy Ashby, Sterling Hitchcock, and, of course, Trevor Hoffman.

Brown finished with an 18–7 record and a 2.38 ERA. Hoffman had his best season. He tied the NL record with 53 saves and only one blown

Kevin Brown helped the Padres reach the World Series in 1998 with a record of 18–7 and a 2.38 ERA.

He began jogging to the mound as the ominous opening riffs of AC/DC's "Hells Bells" played. The batters he faced knew they were in trouble.

After struggling through the 1997 season, Greg Vaughn regained his power stroke and hit 50 home runs. He hit homer number 50 in his final at-bat of the regular season in a victory over the Arizona Diamondbacks. That shot seemed to give the Padres an extra boost as they headed to Houston to open the playoffs against the Astros.

Despite their record of 98–64, the Padres were somewhat disregarded as they entered the playoffs. The Astros and the Atlanta Braves had better records, but the Padres would beat them both to reach the World Series.

Brown set a team record with 16 strikeouts in one game. He won a memorable duel with

opportunity. With his wicked change-up that dropped into the dirt, batters stood no chance. If the Padres took the lead into the ninth inning, Hoffman would come in and slam the door shut. A tradition was born that July when Hoffman chose new entrance music.

Greg Vaughn's 50 home runs for the season helped lift the Padres into the 1998 playoffs.

Houston's Randy Johnson in the NL Division Series opener at the Astrodome. Backed by key home runs from Jim Leyritz and a Hitchcock win against Johnson, the Padres eliminated the Astros in four games. They moved on to the NLCS to face the Atlanta Braves and their talented pitching staff.

Behind Caminiti, Brown, and Hitchcock, the Padres stunned all of baseball by winning the first three games. They outpitched Atlanta's tough trio of starters, John Smoltz, Tom

Glavine, and Greg Maddux. They could not clinch the pennant at home, however. The talented Braves fought back to win two straight games in San Diego. The series returned to Atlanta, where Hitchcock had perhaps his biggest moment. He struck out eight and pitched five innings of two-hit ball to beat the Braves 5–0. The victory sent the Padres to the World Series. The Padres headed out to the pitcher's mound for a team photo to commemorate the event. For his two victories, Hitchcock was named the MVP of the NLCS. Back in San Diego, revelers partied all across the city.

Unfortunately for the Padres, that would be the

Padres Wally Joyner, *left*, Trevor Hoffman, *center*, and Carlos Hernandez, *right*, celebrate their 1998 NLCS victory against the Atlanta Braves.

SNUBBED TWICE

Trevor Hoffman twice finished second in the voting for the NL Cy Young Award, in 1998 and again in 2006. The snub in 1998 was particularly unexpected because Hoffman had tied the NL record with 53 saves. He was a big reason why the Padres reached the World Series. The voting was announced, and Atlanta starter Tom Glavine won the award.

Afterward, it was revealed that Hoffman's name did not even appear on the ballots of six of the 32 voters. Some of those voters later said they did not think a reliever deserved to be considered for the award. Six years later, Hoffman finished second to Arizona Diamondbacks starter Brandon Webb. Webb was 16–8 with a 3.10 ERA. Hoffman had an outstanding season himself, with an NL–best 46 saves and a 2.14 ERA. He left for the Milwaukee Brewers in 2009.

season's high point. They headed to New York for a World Series showdown with the mighty Yankees. New York had won 114 games in the regular season, an AL record. The Padres hushed the rowdy Yankee Stadium crowd by taking a 5–2 lead in Game 1. Two home runs by Vaughn and a solo shot by Tony Gwynn led the way.

Slugger Vaughn

Greg Vaughn helped the Padres win two division titles and one NL pennant with his power hitting. He was acquired late in the 1996 season in a trade with the Milwaukee Brewers. He struggled mightily in 1997. His batting average tumbled to .216 and he hit only 18 home runs. He bounced back in 1998 with a .272 average and a club-record 50 home runs. His 50th home run came in the final game of the regular season. It seemed to give the Padres a spark heading into their playoff series against the Houston Astros. Vaughn also homered in the playoff opener. He hit two homers in Game 1 of the World Series at Yankee Stadium.

But Brown was knocked out of the game with an injury, and the Yankees rallied. The big blow was a grand slam by Tino Martinez. The homer carried the Yankees to a 9–6 win in front of their frenzied fans.

The Padres lost the next night in Yankee Stadium and never recovered. They had a lead in Game 3 in San Diego, giving Padres fans hope. That disappeared, however, when Scott Brosius hit a three-run home run off Hoffman for a 5–4 win. The Yankees wrapped up the championship the next night against Brown. Once the Yankees moved their celebration from the field to the clubhouse, the Padres players returned to the field. They received a rousing standing ovation from the fans. Some players, such as first baseman Wally Joyner, scooped up dirt from the pitcher's mound.

Padres pitcher Sterling Hitchcock salutes the stands during Game 3 of the 1998 World Series.

A few days later, the Padres were honored with a parade through downtown San Diego.

The lasting legacy of that 1998 World Series is Petco Park. Less than two weeks after the Series ended, voters approved a new downtown ballpark. The Padres had been pushing for a new ballpark since the moment Moores bought the team. The measure won easily.

CHAPTER 6

PETCO PARK
AND BEYOND

Padres fans felt good about their team despite the sweep by the Yankees. Within weeks, though, the front office began dismantling the team. Management wanted to save money while the new ballpark was built. Kevin Brown, Ken Caminiti, and Steve Finley left as free agents. Pitcher Joey Hamilton and left fielder Greg Vaughn were traded.

The Padres remained at Qualcomm Stadium for five dismal seasons before moving downtown. The team was not very good, posting five straight losing seasons. The worst was an ugly 64–98 record in 2003 during their last year at Qualcomm.

The 2001 season was both difficult and entertaining. The Padres were no-hit twice, first by A. J. Burnett of the Florida Marlins and then by Bud Smith of the St. Louis Cardinals. On the other hand, Rickey Henderson was back with the club. It would turn out to be a

Rickey Henderson received this gold-plated commemorative home plate when he broke Ty Cobb's record for career runs scored in 2001.

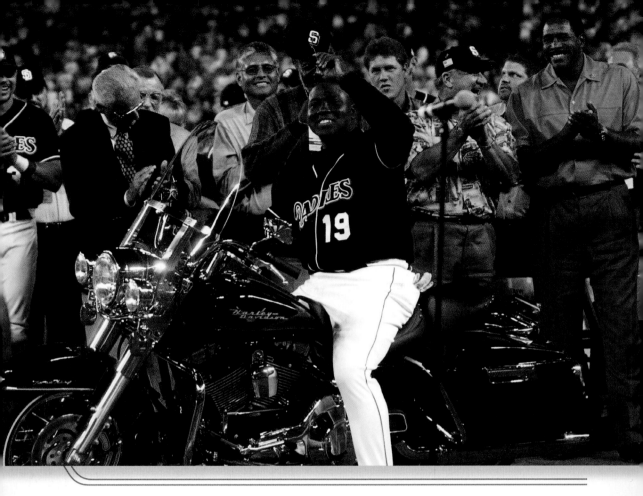

Tony Gwynn's teammates gave him this motorcycle at his retirement ceremony.

record-breaking season for the popular leadoff hitter. Henderson broke Babe Ruth's record for career walks, broke Ty Cobb's career record for runs scored, and got his 3,000th hit on the last day of the season. He celebrated breaking Cobb's record by sliding into home feetfirst rather than his usual headfirst slide.

It was also Tony Gwynn's farewell season. After 20 years, his knees were shot. He had been reduced to mostly pinch-hitting. He had also taken a job as baseball coach at his alma mater, San Diego State.

The original schedule had the Padres playing the final week on the road. Because of the September 11 terrorist attacks, a week's worth of home games were postponed and added to the end of the season. That meant Padres fans got to say good-bye to Gwynn in person. His final appearance in a Padres uniform came on October 7, 2001. As the sellout crowd stood and cheered, he grounded out to shortstop as a pinch-hitter.

The next five years would offer a few highlights. In 2002, right-hander Jake Peavy made a brilliant debut against the New York Yankees. Although he did not win that day, he was in the big leagues to stay. Peavy would become San Diego's ace and win the NL Cy Young Award in 2007.

The move to Petco Park at the start of the 2004 season brought the Padres full circle. The PCL Padres had once played just up the road from the new ballpark.

Construction on Petco Park was delayed for two years because of several lawsuits. Petco Park was the product of a partnership between the Padres

Jake Peavy

One of the most exciting Padres in recent seasons was right-hander Jake Peavy. He led the Padres to consecutive playoff appearances in 2005 and 2006. He was the unanimous choice for the NL Cy Young Award in 2007 after going 19–6 while leading the majors with a 2.54 ERA and 240 strikeouts. Peavy was impressive from the first minute he stepped onto a major league mound. He faced the New York Yankees on June 22, 2002, at Qualcomm Stadium. Then 21, Peavy gave up only three hits in six innings in the 1–0 loss. Peavy led the NL in ERA in 2004 and strikeouts in 2005. He received a $52 million contract extension in 2007—the biggest deal in team history. Less than two years later, he was traded to the Chicago White Sox during the 2009 season.

Ryan Klesko, *right*, and Phil Nevin celebrate Nevin's two-run home run on June 29, 2000, against the Los Angeles Dodgers.

and two government agencies, including the city of San Diego. The public agencies contributed $303.8 million, while the Padres put in $153 million. The city owns 70 percent and the Padres own 30 percent.

Initially, sluggers Phil Nevin and Ryan Klesko complained about the field. They worried that the spacious outfield would gobble up fly balls that would be home runs in other ballparks. Nonetheless, the Padres were 87–75 in their first season at Petco. It was their first winning record since their 1998 World Series season. The Padres returned to the playoffs in 2005, when they won the NL West at 82–80. They were swept in the playoffs by the St. Louis Cardinals.

San Diego won the division again in 2006, and once again faced the Cardinals in the playoffs. This time, they lost in four games. Manager Bruce Bochy was forced out after that season and was replaced by Bud Black. San Diego came within one game of making it to the playoffs. It would have been a team-record third straight year. They played a 163rd game to decide the 2007 NL wild card. The Padres lost to the Rockies in Colorado in an epic 13-inning showdown. In 2007, Gwynn earned national recognition when he was elected into the Hall of Fame.

The Padres lost 99 games to finish last in the NL West in 2008. The next season was another year of transition. The

ALL-STAR HITTER

The Padres acquired Adrian Gonzalez from the Texas Rangers prior to the 2006 season. Born in San Diego, Gonzalez was the number one pick overall by the Florida Marlins in the 2000 amateur draft. He was traded to Texas during the 2003 season. He blossomed once he was back home in San Diego. An injury to Ryan Klesko allowed Gonzalez to become the starter at first base, and he began swatting home runs at Petco Park. Although other left-handers have complained about Petco Park's deep outfield, Gonzo hits home runs to all fields. The smooth-fielding first baseman was named to the All-Star team three straight seasons from 2008 to 2010. He also won Gold Glove Awards in the first two of those seasons. Gonzalez was traded to the Boston Red Sox after the 2010 season.

Adrian Gonzalez hit 31 home runs and had 101 RBIs in 2010.

Padres traded Peavy to the Chicago White Sox for four pitchers.

San Diego had an impressive finish in 2009. The team won 37 of its final 62 games, taking fourth place in the NL West. Heath Bell led the NL in saves with 42. The Padres were led by veterans Adrian Gonzalez and David Eckstein, as well as younger players Nick Hundley, Will Venable, Chase Headley, and Gwynn's son, Tony Jr.

The Padres came painfully close to the playoffs in 2010. They led the NL West for much of the season. Mat Latos was one of three Padres pitchers to win 14 games. Their season ended with an exciting showdown against the San Francisco Giants. The Padres kept their hopes alive with two straight wins, but lost the final game and were eliminated. Despite the disappointment, the Padres finished 90–72.

The 2011 season proved challenging. The team got off to a slow start. Key players suffered injuries. Ending with a 71–91 record, the Padres took fifth place in the NL West.

In 2012, the Padres had a slightly higher record, at 76–86.

Headley led the NL in RBIs, at 115. He also earned his first Gold Glove and Silver Slugger awards.

The 2013 season started with a 5–15 record. Then things started looking up. The team tied for third place in the NL West, with a 76–86 record again. Although the Padres have fallen short of the playoffs in recent years, they showed signs that good things lay ahead.

TIMELINE

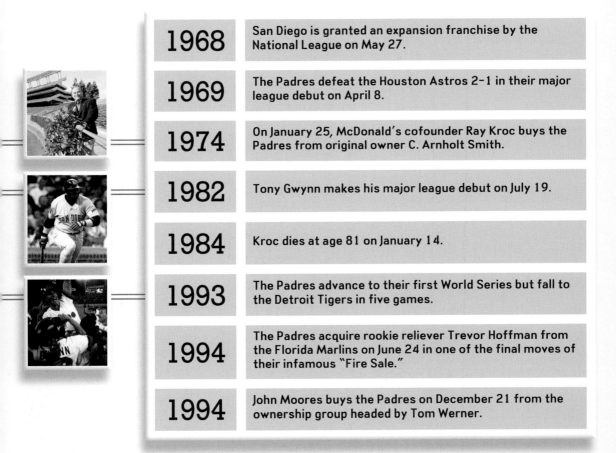

1968	San Diego is granted an expansion franchise by the National League on May 27.
1969	The Padres defeat the Houston Astros 2-1 in their major league debut on April 8.
1974	On January 25, McDonald's cofounder Ray Kroc buys the Padres from original owner C. Arnholt Smith.
1982	Tony Gwynn makes his major league debut on July 19.
1984	Kroc dies at age 81 on January 14.
1993	The Padres advance to their first World Series but fall to the Detroit Tigers in five games.
1994	The Padres acquire rookie reliever Trevor Hoffman from the Florida Marlins on June 24 in one of the final moves of their infamous "Fire Sale."
1994	John Moores buys the Padres on December 21 from the ownership group headed by Tom Werner.

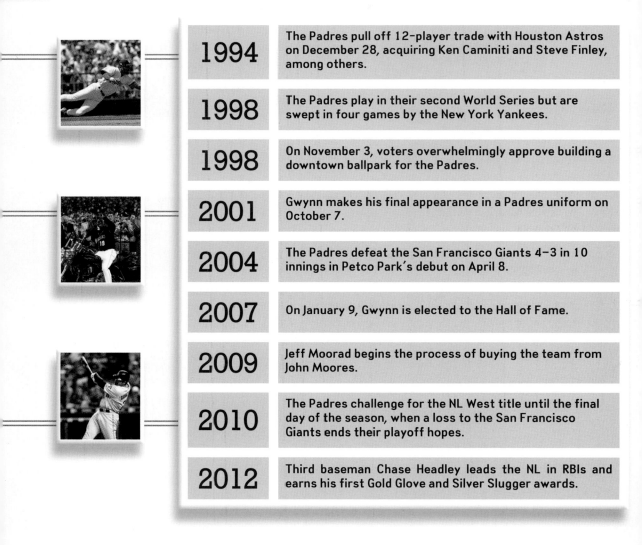

1994	The Padres pull off 12-player trade with Houston Astros on December 28, acquiring Ken Caminiti and Steve Finley, among others.
1998	The Padres play in their second World Series but are swept in four games by the New York Yankees.
1998	On November 3, voters overwhelmingly approve building a downtown ballpark for the Padres.
2001	Gwynn makes his final appearance in a Padres uniform on October 7.
2004	The Padres defeat the San Francisco Giants 4–3 in 10 innings in Petco Park's debut on April 8.
2007	On January 9, Gwynn is elected to the Hall of Fame.
2009	Jeff Moorad begins the process of buying the team from John Moores.
2010	The Padres challenge for the NL West title until the final day of the season, when a loss to the San Francisco Giants ends their playoff hopes.
2012	Third baseman Chase Headley leads the NL in RBIs and earns his first Gold Glove and Silver Slugger awards.

QUICK STATS

FRANCHISE HISTORY

San Diego Padres (1969–)

WORLD SERIES

1984, 1998

NL CHAMPIONSHIP SERIES

1984, 1998

DIVISION CHAMPIONSHIPS

1984, 1996, 1998, 2005, 2006

WILD-CARD BERTHS

None

KEY PLAYERS
(position[s]; seasons with team)

Heath Bell (RP; 2007–2011)
Andy Benes (SP; 1989–95)
Kevin Brown (SP; 1998)

Ken Caminiti (3B; 1995–98)
Nate Colbert (INF/OF; 1969–74)
Rollie Fingers (RP; 1977–80)
Adrian Gonzalez (1B; 2006–10)
Rich "Goose" Gossage (RP; 1984–87)
Tony Gwynn (OF; 1982–2001)
Chase Headley (3B, 2007–)
Trevor Hoffman (RP; 1993–2008)
Randy Jones (SP; 1973–80)
Mat Latos (SP; 2009–2011)
Jake Peavy (SP; 2002–09)
Benito Santiago (C; 1986–92)
Gary Sheffield (3B; 1992–93)
Chris Young (SP; 2006–2010)

KEY MANAGERS

Bud Black (2007–):
    317–332
Bruce Bochy (1995–2006):
    951–975; 8–16 (postseason)
Dick Williams (1982–85):
    337–311; 4–6 (postseason)

HOME PARKS

San Diego Stadium
    Known as Jack Murphy Stadium
    (1981–96)
    Known as Qualcomm Stadium
    (1997–2003)
Petco Park (2004–)

*All statistics through 2013 season

QUOTES AND ANECDOTES

Injuries and illness did not stop Ken Caminiti during his NL MVP season of 1996. Not only did he play most of the season with a torn rotator cuff, but he had a remarkable performance on August 18 in the steaming heat of Monterrey, Mexico. The Padres were wrapping up a three-game series against the New York Mets when Caminiti showed up at the ballpark suffering from dehydration and an upset stomach. He took two bags of intravenous fluid, ate a Snickers candy bar, then hit two home runs and drove in four runs in an 8–0 victory. The next night in San Diego, he hit a grand slam in a victory over the Montreal Expos. Two nights later, he homered from both sides of the plate for the sixth time in his career.

"We got close. It was special because of you guys."
—Padres first baseman Wally Joyner to the Qualcomm Stadium crowd after the New York Yankees completed a sweep of the 1998 World Series against San Diego

When the Rolling Stones played Petco Park in November 2005, Mick Jagger gave Padres left-hander David Wells a shout-out. "I told management you'd be careful with the sacred dirt of Petco Park, or else David Wells may never return," Jagger told the crowd between songs. It turns out that Wells met the singer a few years earlier.

GLOSSARY

ace

A team's best starting pitcher.

acquire

To add a player, usually through the draft, free agency, or a trade.

berth

A place, spot, or position, such as in the baseball playoffs.

clinch

To officially settle something, such as a berth in the playoffs.

closer

A relief pitcher who is called on to pitch, usually in the ninth inning, to protect his team's lead.

draft

A system used by professional sports leagues to select new players in order to spread incoming talent among all teams.

expansion

In sports, the addition of a franchise or franchises to a league.

franchise

An entire sports organization, including the players, coaches, and staff.

free agent

A player whose contract has expired and who is able to sign with a team of his choice.

friars

Members of a religious order who live in monasteries; monks.

general manager

The executive who is in charge of the team's overall operation. He or she hires and fires managers and coaches, drafts players, and signs free agents.

pennant

A flag. In baseball, it symbolizes that a team has won its league championship.

veteran

An individual with great experience in a particular endeavor.

FOR MORE INFORMATION

Further Reading

Chandler, Bob. *Bob Chandler's Tales from the San Diego Padres.* Champaign, IL: Sports Pub., 2006.

Swank, Bill. *Baseball in San Diego: From the Padres to Petco.* Charleston, SC: Arcadia, 2004.

Vecsey, George. *Baseball: A History of America's Favorite Game.* New York: Modern Library, 2008.

Web Links

To learn more about Inside MLB, visit **booklinks.abdopublishing.com**. These links are routinely monitored and updated to provide the most current information available.

Places to Visit

National Baseball Hall of Fame and Museum
25 Main Street
Cooperstown, NY 13326
1-888-HALL-OF-FAME
http://baseballhall.org
This hall of fame and museum highlights the greatest players and moments in the history of baseball. Tony Gwynn, Dave Winfield, and Rickey Henderson are among the former Padres enshrined here.

Peoria Sports Complex
16101 N. 83rd Ave
Peoria, AZ 85382
623-773-8700
http://sandiego.padres.mlb.com/spring_training/home.jsp?c_id=sd
Located in the Phoenix area, Peoria Sports Complex has been the spring-training home of the Padres since 1994.

Petco Park
100 Park Boulevard
San Diego, CA 92101
619-795-5000
http://sandiego.padres.mlb.com/sd/ballpark/index.jsp
Petco Park has been the Padres' home field since 2004. Tours are available when the Padres are not playing.

INDEX

About the Author

Bernie Wilson has worked for The Associated Press since 1984. He has covered Major League Baseball on a regular basis since 1988, beginning with the Angels and Dodgers, and has covered the San Diego Padres since 1991. He also covers the San Diego Chargers, San Diego State, and the America's Cup and has covered seven Olympics.